COMFORT

AT HOME IN
GOD'S LOVE

COMFORT: AT HOME IN GOD'S LOVE

COPYRIGHT © 1996 BY GARBORG'S HEART 'N HOME, INC.

PUBLISHED BY GARBORG'S HEART 'N HOME, INC.

P.O. BOX 20132, BLOOMINGTON, MN 55420

ALL TEXT IN THIS BOOK HAS BEEN TAKEN FROM *THE MESSAGE* © BY
EUGENE H. PETERSON, 1996. ALL RIGHTS RESERVED. PUBLISHED BY PERMISSION
OF NAVPRESS, P.O. BOX 35001, COLORADO SPRINGS, CO 80933, AND IN
ASSOCIATION WITH THE LITERARY AGENCY OF ALIVE COMMUNICATIONS, INC.,
1465 KELLY JOHNSON BLVD., SUITE 320, COLORADO SPRINGS, CO 80920.

ART: SCALA/ART RESOURCE, NY

ANCILLOTTI, TORELLO. *SUNSET.*

GALLERIA D'ARTE MODERNA, FLORENCE, ITALY.

ISBN 1-881830-35-7

COMFORT

AT HOME IN
GOD'S LOVE

The Message is a contemporary rendering of the Bible from
the original languages, crafted to present its tone, rhythm,
events, and ideas in everyday speech.

GOD IS
THERE,
READY
TO HELP

$\mathcal{S}$ince God assured us, "I'll never let you
down, never walk off and leave you,"
we can boldly quote,
"God is there, ready to help."

■ ■ ■ ■ ■ ■ ■ ■ ■ ■ ■ ■ ■ ■

Hebrews 13:5-6

COMFORT

$\mathscr{I}$s anyone crying for help?
GOD is listening,
ready to rescue you.
If your heart is broken,
you'll find GOD right there.

■ ■ ■ ■ ■ ■ ■ ■ ■ ■ ■ ■ ■ ■

Psalm 34:17-18

COMFORT

*J*esus resumed talking to the people, but now tenderly..."Come to me. Get away with me and you'll recover your life. I'll show you how to take a real rest. Walk with me and work with me—watch how I do it. Learn the unforced rhythms of grace. I won't lay anything heavy or ill-fitting on you. Keep company with me and you'll learn to live freely and lightly."

■ ■ ■ ■ ■ ■ ■ ■ ■ ■ ■ ■ ■ ■

Matthew 11:27-30

COMFORT

$\mathcal{P}$ile your troubles on GOD's shoulders—
he'll carry your load, he'll help you out.

■ ■ ■ ■ ■ ■ ■ ■ ■ ■ ■ ■ ■ ■

Psalm 55:22

COMFORT

By entering through faith into what God has always wanted to do for us—set us right with him, make us fit for him—we have it all together with God because of our Master Jesus. And that's not all: We throw open our doors to God and discover at the same moment that he has already thrown open his door to us. We find ourselves standing where we always hoped we might stand—out in the wide open spaces of God's grace and glory, standing tall and shouting our praise.

COMFORT

There's more to come: We continue to shout our praise even when we're hemmed in with troubles, because we know how troubles can develop passionate patience in us, and how that patience in turn forges the tempered steel of virtue, keeping us alert for whatever God will do next.

Romans 5:1-5

■ ■ ■ ■ ■ ■ ■ ■ ■ ■ ■ ■ ■ ■

COMFORT

$\mathcal{Y}$ou're blessed when you feel you've lost what is most dear to you. Only then can you be embraced by the One most dear to you.... You're blessed when you care. At the moment of being "care-full," you find yourselves cared for.

■ ■ ■ ■ ■ ■ ■ ■ ■ ■ ■ ■ ■ ■

Matthew 5:4,7

COMFORT

$\mathcal{O}$pen your mouth and taste, open your eyes
and see—how good GOD is.
Blessed are you who run to him.

■ ■ ■ ■ ■ ■ ■ ■ ■ ■ ■ ■ ■ ■

Psalm 34:8

COMFORT

What a beautiful thing, GOD, to give thanks,
to sing an anthem to you, the High God!
To announce your love each daybreak,
sing your faithful presence all through the night.

■ ■ ■ ■ ■ ■ ■ ■ ■ ■ ■ ■ ■

Psalm 92:1-2

COMFORT

COMFORT

The deeper your love, the higher it goes;
every cloud is a flag to your faithfulness.
Soar high in the skies, O God!
Cover the whole earth with your glory!

■ ■ ■ ■ ■ ■ ■ ■ ■ ■ ■ ■ ■ ■

Psalm 57:10-11

COMFORT

$\mathscr{B}$ut you, O God, are both tender and kind,
not easily angered, immense in love,
and you never, never quit.

■ ■ ■ ■ ■ ■ ■ ■ ■ ■ ■ ■ ■ ■

Psalm 86:15

COMFORT

Jesus was quick to comfort them:
"Courage! It's me. Don't be afraid."

■ ■ ■ ■ ■ ■ ■ ■ ■ ■ ■ ■ ■

Mark 6:50

COMFORT

$\mathcal{H}$ow blessed is God! And what a blessing he is! He's the Father of our Master, Jesus Christ, and takes us to the high places of blessing in him. Long before he laid down earth's foundations, he had us in mind, had settled on us as the focus of his love.

Ephesians 1:3-4

COMFORT

$\mathcal{M}$y grace is enough; it's all you need.
My strength comes into its own
in your weakness.

■ ■ ■ ■ ■ ■ ■ ■ ■ ■ ■ ■ ■ ■

2 Corinthians 12:9

$\mathcal{G}$od's love...is ever and always,
eternally present to all who fear him.

■ ■ ■ ■ ■ ■ ■ ■ ■ ■ ■ ■ ■ ■

Psalm 103:17

COMFORT

So we're not giving up. How could we! Even though on the outside it often looks like things are falling apart on us, on the inside, where God is making new life, not a day goes by without his unfolding grace.... There's far more here than meets the eye. The things we see now are here today, gone tomorrow. But the things we can't see now will last forever.

■■■■■■■■■■■■■■

2 Corinthians 4:16-18

COMFORT

TAKE
HEART!

$\mathcal{I}$'ve told you all this so that trusting me, you will be unshakable and assured, deeply at peace. In this godless world you will continue to experience difficulties. But take heart! I've conquered the world.

■ ■ ■ ■ ■ ■ ■ ■ ■ ■ ■ ■ ■ ■

John 16:33

COMFORT

All praise to the God and Father of our Master, Jesus the Messiah! Father of all mercy! God of all healing counsel! He comes alongside us when we go through hard times, and before you know it, he brings us alongside someone else who is going through hard times so that we can be there for that person just as God was there for us.

■ ■ ■ ■ ■ ■ ■ ■ ■ ■ ■ ■ ■ ■

2 Corinthians 1:3-4

COMFORT

What a God we have! And how fortunate we are to have him, this Father of our Master Jesus! Because Jesus was raised from the dead, we've been given a brand-new life and have everything to live for, including a future in heaven—and the future starts now! God is keeping careful watch over us and the future. The Day is coming when you'll have it all— life healed and whole.

COMFORT

I know how great this makes you feel, even
though you have to put up with every kind of
aggravation in the meantime. Pure gold put in
the fire comes out of it *proved* pure; genuine
faith put through this suffering comes
out *proved* genuine.

■ ■ ■ ■ ■ ■ ■ ■ ■ ■ ■ ■ ■

1 Peter 1:3-7

COMFORT

*E*veryone's going through a refining fire
sooner or later, but you'll be well-preserved,
protected from the *eternal* flames.

■ ■ ■ ■ ■ ■ ■ ■ ■ ■ ■ ■ ■

Mark 9:49-50

COMFORT

*I*f each grain of sand on
the seashore were numbered
and the sum labeled "chosen of God,"
they'd be numbers still, not names;
salvation comes by personal selection.
God doesn't count us; he calls us by name.

■ ■ ■ ■ ■ ■ ■ ■ ■ ■ ■ ■ ■ ■

Romans 9:27

COMFORT

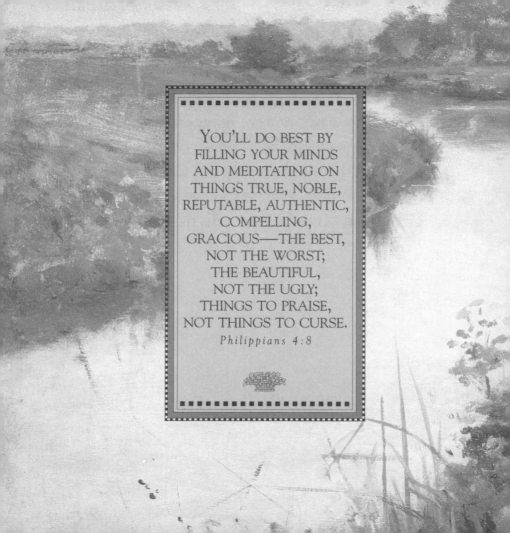

You'll do best by filling your minds and meditating on things true, noble, reputable, authentic, compelling, gracious—the best, not the worst; the beautiful, not the ugly; things to praise, not things to curse.

Philippians 4:8

$\mathcal{W}$e can only keep on going, after all, by the power of God, who first saved us and then called us.... We had nothing to do with it. It was all *his* idea, a gift prepared for us in Jesus long before we knew anything about it.... Death defeated, life vindicated in a steady blaze of light, all through the work of Jesus.

■ ■ ■ ■ ■ ■ ■ ■ ■ ■ ■ ■ ■ ■

2 Timothy 1:8-10

COMFORT

$\mathcal{C}$onsider it a sheer gift, friends, when tests
and challenges come at you from all sides. You
know that under pressure, your faith-life is
forced into the open and shows its true colors.
So don't try to get out of anything prematurely.
Let it do its work so you become mature and
well-developed, not deficient in any way.

▪ ▪ ▪ ▪ ▪ ▪ ▪ ▪ ▪ ▪ ▪ ▪ ▪

James 1:2-4

COMFORT

We pray that you'll have the strength to stick it out over the long haul—not the grim strength of gritting your teeth but the glory-strength God gives. It is strength that endures the unendurable and spills over into joy, thanking the Father who makes us strong enough to take part in everything bright and beautiful that he has for us.

■ ■ ■ ■ ■ ■ ■ ■ ■ ■ ■ ■ ■ ■ ■

Colossians 1:11-12

COMFORT

I look up to the mountains;
does my strength come from mountains?
No, my strength comes from GOD,
who made heaven, and earth, and mountains.
He won't let you stumble,
your Guardian God won't fall asleep.

■ ■ ■ ■ ■ ■ ■ ■ ■ ■ ■ ■ ■

Psalm 121:1-3

COMFORT

$\mathcal{G}$OD guards you from every evil,
he guards your very life.
He guards you when you leave and
when you return,
he guards you now, he guards you always.

■ ■ ■ ■ ■ ■ ■ ■ ■ ■ ■ ■ ■ ■

Psalm 121:7-8

COMFORT

The spacious, free life is from GOD,
it's also protected and safe.
GOD-strengthened, we're delivered from evil—
when we run to him, he saves us.

■■■■■■■■■■■■■■■

Psalm 37:39-40

Our Lord is great, with limitless strength;
we'll never comprehend what he knows and does.
GOD puts the fallen on their feet again...
He launches his promises earthward—
how swift and sure they come!

■■■■■■■■■■■■■

Psalm 147:5-6,15

COMFORT

I cherish your commandments—
oh, how I love them!—
relishing every fragment of your counsel.
Remember what you said to me, your servant—
I hang on to these words for dear life!
These words hold me up in bad times;
yes, your promises rejuvenate me.

■ ■ ■ ■ ■ ■ ■ ■ ■ ■ ■ ■ ■ ■

Psalm 119:47-50

COMFORT

$\mathscr{I}$'m sure now I'll see God's goodness
in the exuberant earth.
Stay with GOD!
Take heart. Don't quit.

■ ■ ■ ■ ■ ■ ■ ■ ■ ■ ■ ■ ■ ■

Psalm 27:13-14

COMFORT

FAITH IS
OUR
HANDLE

The fundamental fact of existence is that this trust in God, this faith, is the firm foundation under everything that makes life worth living. It's our handle on what we can't see.

■■■■■■■■■■■■■■

Hebrews 11:1,3

COMFORT

$\mathscr{I}$t's what we trust in but don't
yet see that keeps us going.

■ ■ ■ ■ ■ ■ ■ ■ ■ ■ ■ ■ ■ ■

2 Corinthians 5:7

COMFORT

We know only a portion of the truth, and what we say about God is always incomplete. But when the Complete arrives, our incompletes will be canceled....

We don't yet see things clearly. We're squinting in a fog, peering through a mist. But it won't be long before the weather clears and the sun shines bright! We'll see it all then, see it all as clearly as God sees us, knowing him directly just as he knows us!

COMFORT

But for right now, until that completeness, we
have three things to do to lead us toward that
consummation: Trust steadily in God,
hope unswervingly, love extravagantly.
And the best of the three is love.

■ ■ ■ ■ ■ ■ ■ ■ ■ ■ ■ ■ ■

1 Corinthians 13:9-13

COMFORT

$\mathcal{M}$ake sure I'm fit
inside and out
So I never lose
sight of your love,
But keep in step with you.

■ ■ ■ ■ ■ ■ ■ ■ ■ ■ ■ ■ ■ ■ ■

Psalm 26:2-3

COMFORT

*G*od's Word vaults across the skies
from sunrise to sunset,
Melting ice, scorching deserts,
warming hearts to faith.
The revelation of GOD is whole
and pulls our lives together.
The signposts of GOD are clear
and point out the right road.
The life-maps of GOD are right,
showing the way to joy.

■ ■ ■ ■ ■ ■ ■ ■ ■ ■ ■ ■ ■ ■

Psalm 19:6-8

COMFORT

With your very own hands you formed me;
now breathe your wisdom over me
so I can understand you.
When they see me waiting,
expecting your Word,
those who fear you will take heart and be glad.
I can see now, GOD, that your
decisions are right;

COMFORT

Your testing has taught me what's
true and right.
Oh, love me—and right now!—hold me tight!
just the way you promised.
Now comfort me so I can live, really live;
your revelation is the tune I dance to.

■ ■ ■ ■ ■ ■ ■ ■ ■ ■ ■ ■ ■ ■

Psalm 119:73-77

COMFORT

I'm staying on your trail;
I'm putting one foot
In front of the other.
I'm not giving up.
I call to you, God, because
I'm sure of an answer....
Keep your eye on me;
hide me under your cool wing feathers.

■ ■ ■ ■ ■ ■ ■ ■ ■ ■ ■ ■ ■ ■

Psalm 17:5-6,8

COMFORT

COMFORT

God, my shepherd!
I don't need a thing.
You have bedded me down in lush meadows,
you find me quiet pools to drink from.
True to your word,
you let me catch my breath
and send me in the right direction.

Even when the way goes
through Death Valley,
I'm not afraid
when you walk at my side.
Your trusty shepherd's crook
makes me feel secure.

■ ■ ■ ■ ■ ■ ■ ■ ■ ■ ■ ■ ■

Psalm 23:1-4

COMFORT

God's eye is on those who respect him,
the ones who are looking for his love.
He's ready to come to their rescue in bad times;
in lean times he keeps body and soul together.

COMFORT

We're depending on GOD;
he's everything we need....
Love us, GOD, with all you've got—
that's what we're depending on.

■ ■ ■ ■ ■ ■ ■ ■ ■ ■ ■ ■ ■ ■

Psalm 33:18-20,22

COMFORT

You, who made me stare trouble in the face,
Turn me around;
Now let me look life in the face.
I've been to the bottom;

COMFORT

Bring me up, streaming with honors;
turn to me, be tender to me,
And I'll take up the lute and thank you
to the tune of your faithfulness, God.

■ ■ ■ ■ ■ ■ ■ ■ ■ ■ ■ ■ ■ ■

Psalm 71:20-22

COMFORT

AT HOME IN GOD'S LOVE

I've loved you the way my Father
has loved me. Make yourselves
at home in my love.

∎∎∎∎∎∎∎∎∎∎∎∎∎∎

John 15:9

COMFORT

*G*od's love is meteoric,
his loyalty astronomic,
his purpose titanic,
his verdicts oceanic.
Yet in his largeness
nothing gets lost.

■ ■ ■ ■ ■ ■ ■ ■ ■ ■ ■ ■ ■ ■

Psalm 36:5-6

COMFORT

I call to GOD,
I cry to God to help me.
From his palace he hears my call;
my cry brings me right into his presence—
a private audience!...

COMFORT

God stuck by me.
He stood me up on a wide-open field;
I stood there saved—surprised to be loved!
God made my life complete
when I placed all the pieces before him....
God rewrote the text of my life
when I opened the book of my heart
to his eyes.

Psalm 18:6,18-20,24

COMFORT

As parents feel for their children,
GOD feels for those who fear him.
He knows us inside and out,
keeps in mind that we're made of mud.

■ ■ ■ ■ ■ ■ ■ ■ ■ ■ ■ ■ ■ ■

Psalm 103:13-14

COMFORT

It's in Christ that we find out who we are
and what we are living for. Long before we first
heard of Christ and got our hopes up, he had
his eye on us, had designs on us for glorious
living, part of the overall purpose he is working
out in everything and everyone.

■ ■ ■ ■ ■ ■ ■ ■ ■ ■ ■ ■ ■ ■

Ephesians 1:11

COMFORT

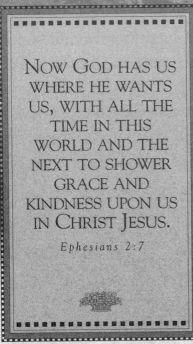

NOW GOD HAS US
WHERE HE WANTS
US, WITH ALL THE
TIME IN THIS
WORLD AND THE
NEXT TO SHOWER
GRACE AND
KINDNESS UPON US
IN CHRIST JESUS.

Ephesians 2:7

*H*e knows us far better than we know ourselves, knows our...condition, and keeps us present before God. That's why we can be so sure that every detail in our lives of love for God is worked into something good. God knew what he was doing from the very beginning. He decided from the outset to shape the lives of those who love him along the same lines as the life of his Son....

COMFORT

After God made that decision of what his children should be like, he followed it up by calling people by name. After he called them by name, he set them on a solid basis with himself. And then, after getting them established, he stayed with them to the end, gloriously completing what he had begun....

COMFORT

So, what do you think? With God on our side like this, how can we lose? If God didn't hesitate to put everything on the line for us, embracing our condition and exposing himself to the worst by sending his own Son, is there anything else he wouldn't gladly and freely do for us? And who would dare tangle with God by messing with one of God's chosen? Who would dare even to point a finger?

COMFORT

The One who died for us—who was raised to life for us!—is in the presence of God at this very moment sticking up for us. Do you think anyone is going to be able to drive a wedge between us and Christ's love for us? There is no way! Not trouble, not hard times, not hatred, not hunger...not even the worst sins listed in Scripture.

■ ■ ■ ■ ■ ■ ■ ■ ■ ■ ■ ■ ■

Romans 8:27-35

COMFORT

Now that we know what we have—Jesus, this great High Priest with ready access to God—let's not let it slip through our fingers. We don't have a priest who is out of touch with our reality. He's been through weakness and testing, experienced it all—all but the sin. So let's walk right up to him and get what he is so ready to give. Take the mercy, accept the help.

■ ■ ■ ■ ■ ■ ■ ■ ■ ■ ■ ■ ■

Hebrews 4:14-16

COMFORT

$\mathcal{G}$OD is all strength for his people,
ample refuge...
Save your people
and bless your heritage.
Care for them;
carry them like a good shepherd.

▪ ▪ ▪ ▪ ▪ ▪ ▪ ▪ ▪ ▪ ▪ ▪ ▪

Psalm 28:8-9

COMFORT

$\mathscr{T}$he amazing grace of the Master, Jesus
Christ, the extravagant love of God, the
intimate friendship of the Holy Spirit,
be with...you.

■ ■ ■ ■ ■ ■ ■ ■ ■ ■ ■ ■ ■ ■

2 Corinthians 13:14

COMFORT

$\mathcal{G}$OD is all mercy and grace—
not quick to anger, is rich in love.
GOD is good to one and all;
everything he does is suffused with grace.

■ ■ ■ ■ ■ ■ ■ ■ ■ ■ ■ ■ ■ ■

Psalm 145:8-9

COMFORT

JOY
COMES
WITH THE
MORNING

$\mathscr{Y}$ou're blessed when you've lost it all.
God's kingdom is there for the finding....
You're blessed when the tears flow freely.
Joy comes with the morning.

■ ■ ■ ■ ■ ■ ■ ■ ■ ■ ■ ■ ■ ■

Luke 6:20-21

COMFORT

$\mathcal{T}$une me in to foot-tapping songs,
set these once-broken bones to dancing....
God, make a fresh start in me...
put a fresh wind in my sails!

■ ■ ■ ■ ■ ■ ■ ■ ■ ■ ■ ■ ■ ■

Psalm 51:8,10,12

COMFORT

I saw God before me for all time.
Nothing can shake me; he's right by my side.
I'm glad from the inside out, ecstatic;
I've pitched my tent in the land of hope....
You've got my feet on the life-path,
with your face shining sun-joy all around.

■ ■ ■ ■ ■ ■ ■ ■ ■ ■ ■ ■ ■ ■

Acts 2:25-28

COMFORT

Through the heartfelt mercies of our God,
God's Sunrise will break in upon us,
Shining on those in the darkness,
those sitting in the shadow of death,
Then showing us the way, one foot at a time,
down the path of peace.

■ ■ ■ ■ ■ ■ ■ ■ ■ ■ ■ ■ ■ ■

Luke 1:78-79

COMFORT

You protect me with salvation-armor;
you hold me up with a firm hand,
caress me with your gentle ways.
You cleared the ground under me
so my footing was firm.

■ ■ ■ ■ ■ ■ ■ ■ ■ ■ ■ ■ ■ ■

Psalm 18:35-36

COMFORT

$\mathcal{L}$et's keep a firm grip on the promises that keep us going. He always keeps his word.

∎∎∎∎∎∎∎∎∎∎∎∎∎∎∎

Hebrews 10:23

COMFORT

Bless our God, oh peoples!
Give him a thunderous welcome!
Didn't he set us on the road to life?...
He trained us first,
passed us like silver through refining fires...
pushed us to our very limit....
Finally he brought us
to this well-watered place.

■ ■ ■ ■ ■ ■ ■ ■ ■ ■ ■ ■ ■ ■

Psalm 66:8-12

COMFORT

The Spirit of God whets our appetite by giving us a taste of what's ahead. He puts a little of heaven in our hearts so that we'll never settle for less.

■ ■ ■ ■ ■ ■ ■ ■ ■ ■ ■ ■ ■

2 Corinthians 5:5

COMFORT

*O*h, the utter extravagance of his work
in us who trust him—endless energy,
boundless strength!

■ ■ ■ ■ ■ ■ ■ ■ ■ ■ ■ ■ ■ ■

Ephesians 1:19

COMFORT

COMFORT

May God, who puts all things together,
makes all things whole,
Who made a lasting mark through the
sacrifice of Jesus,
the sacrifice of blood that sealed the
eternal covenant,
Who led Jesus, our Great Shepherd,
up and alive from the dead,

COMFORT

Now put you together, provide you
with everything you need to please him,
Make us into what gives him most pleasure,
by means of the sacrifice of Jesus, the Messiah.
All glory to Jesus forever and always!

■ ■ ■ ■ ■ ■ ■ ■ ■ ■ ■ ■ ■ ■

Hebrews 13:20-21

COMFORT

I am, right now, Resurrection and Life.
The one who believes in me, even though he
or she dies, will live. And everyone who lives
believing in me does not ultimately die at all.

■■■■■■■■■■■■■■

John 11:25-26

COMFORT

The Master himself will...come down from heaven and the dead in Christ will rise—they'll go first. Then the rest of us who are still alive at the time will be caught up with them into the clouds to meet the Master. Oh, we'll be walking on air! And then there will be one huge family reunion with the Master. So reassure one another with these words.

■ ■ ■ ■ ■ ■ ■ ■ ■ ■ ■ ■

1 Thessalonians 4:16-18

COMFORT

Oh! May the God of green hope fill you up
with joy, fill you up with peace, so that your
believing lives, filled with the life-giving energy
of the Holy Spirit, will brim over with hope!

■ ■ ■ ■ ■ ■ ■ ■ ■ ■ ■ ■ ■ ■

Romans 15:13

COMFORT

𝒢od be with you. Grace be with you.

■ ■ ■ ■ ■ ■ ■ ■ ■ ■ ■ ■ ■ ■

2 Timothy 4:22

COMFORT